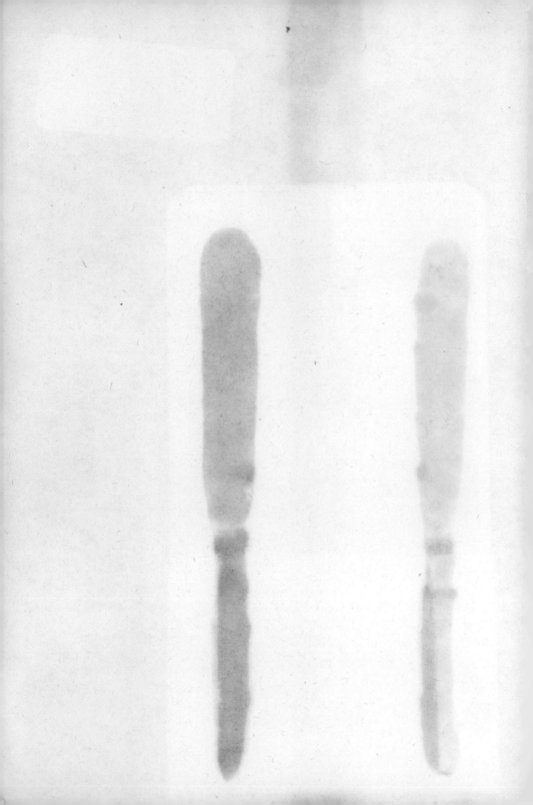

# CLIMB TO THE HIGH COUNTRY

# CLIMB TO THE HIGH COUNTRY

### BILL HOTCHKISS

W · W · NORTON & COMPANY, INC · NEW YORK

A few of these poems have previously appeared in the following publications, to whose editors grateful acknowledgment is made: *Beloit Journal, Hard-Pressed, Nitty-Gritty, Shining Clarity, Sierra Journal, Western Slopes Connection, Robinson Jeffers Newsletter,* and *Contemporary Quarterly.*

Book and binding design by Antonina Krass
Typefaces used are vip Primer and Souvenir
Manufacturing done by Vail-Ballou Press, Inc.

ISBN 0 393 cloth edition
ISBN 0 393 paper edition

1 2 3 4 5 6 7 8 9 0

# CONTENTS

To Judith Shears, my wife

And in memory of Bill Henry Hotchkiss, my father

# PREFACE

From the pinnacle of Goat Rock, one may look eastward to see the long white line of the Sierra Nevada Mountains—and one may imagine high meadows, waterfalls, wind–gnarled trees, glacially–carved spires, silence. And one may dream. One may imagine the figure of John Muir, titan like, striding among the peaks.

I was only a boy when I made my first climb to the high country—Mt. Tallac, on the California side of Lake Tahoe. Two days on a mountain, the great cliffs, the snowbanks melting out, timberline, a diminished sense of human importance, and from the summit the unimagined perspective of the Sierra, of Desolation Valley and of the higher peaks off to the south. And the *wildness*. Surely the rising tide of technological civilization would never reach this watermark.

Muir called these mountains "the range of light," even as the Paiutes called them "Inyo," the dwelling place of a Great Spirit, Numunana, the People Father, whose voice may be heard in the thunder.

The geologic record etched upon Sierra rocks begins some hundreds of millions of years ago and suggests seas which no mariner was ever to sail, seas pushed aside by mountains which no pilgrim was ever to climb, mountains drained by rivers whose waters no human was ever to drink or bathe in. Only the rocks may tell us of vanished tropical forests, vanished races of animals and birds, of floods of volcanic fire and great tides of scouring ice, of warm, shallow seas, and of sudden and violent earthquakes.

Jed Smith crossing the impassable mountains in winter. The discovery of gold. New, human tides washing the range, turning the rocks, working the rivers and the gravel deposits of the ridges. Human scratchings. A boy stares eastward from Goat Rock, dreams.

*Climb to the High Country* is arranged as a two-year progression, a double solar cycle—though the poems themselves were composed over a somewhat longer period. Strict chronology is irrelevant, even as the events of the poet's life are, in themselves, unimportant. Still, I might note that these poems are based on real things and experiences, for otherwise what would be their purpose? More than half a century ago, California's greatest poet—Robinson Jeffers—decided not to tell lies in verse:

> ". . . not to feign any emotion that I did not feel;
> not to pretend to believe in optimism or pessimism,
> or unreversible progress; not to say anything
> because it was popular, or generally accepted, or
> fashionable in intellectual circles, unless I myself
> believed in it; and not to believe easily."

Bill Hotchkiss

April 10, 1977
Woodpecker Ravine
Nevada County, California

# CLIMB TO THE HIGH COUNTRY

# WITNESS OF CREATION

I cannot tell you what it was.

Some urging prompted by incipient storm,
The distant growlings of massed summer storm clouds—
Or even what drew me to the campsite between two lakes
In a gouged trench-valley at the headwaters
Of the Mokelumne and the Stanislaus, one flowing north,
The other south, down through raw granite canyons.

Flashes of rain in the wine-like air.

Wind and a light rain, black billowed clouds
Growling and coughing above the Sierras—
Electricity charged on the air. Late August,
But winter, too early, coiled like a rattlesnake.

A man and his dog: and heaped, swirling clouds
Foreboding and numinous
Above the far-reaching sprawl of red-gray peaks.

We ascended the ridge, thick stands of lodgepole
And fir, breaking off at the crest, sharp rocks, bunch grass,
Blues, yellows, whites, reds, the spring flowers
Of the high country that endure their brief season
Where late thaw is followed in a few weeks by winter.

Then the clouds closed to the north, over Reynolds Peak
And Silver Mountain, dense, dark bands of rain and hail
Wind-blown, white slivers of lightning—and the shouts of God.

A terror of beauty:

*Numunana! Numunana lives in the Inyo!*

Was I called to witness this afterlash of creation?

Over the high ridge, down
To a gray-blue tarn
In the gouge at the foot of the talus slope,
At the verge of the scree, where a band of lush grass,
Green amid white stones and dwarfed pines,
And slender, flame-like hemlocks
Made refuge for birds—and a dog and a man.

*In the Inyo! Numunana in the Inyo!*

I rested awhile, uncertain. Studied the long slope
Above me, the jagged, curved peak, gray-silver, stark,
The sheer, heavy rock broken and faulted:
And air like wine and charged with long waves of thunder.

A man and a dog: we climbed upward,
Slowly, carefully, resting often,
To the knife-spine of the mountain—
And there, warned by the gustings of wind,
We huddled by an outcropping arched over
With twisted hemlock and juniper of timberline.

Some minutes of downpour, rain mixed with hail.

When it ceased, we climbed onward;
The terrible energy, vast forces of mountain and cloud,
Discharges of pent-up force, the long roarings—
Like a cleansing and purification, a holiness,
No human thought, no world whatsoever but this one,
Pure as the faint, damp smell of purple penstemon
Flaring bloodstains between broken rocks.

All time was one time—
No past and no future—

To have passed beyond one's own mind,
To have passed down to the animal essence,
Aware, alert, breathing the moist air
Of the beginnings and endings of all things,
My own life utterly incidental to all things,
So purged of human concern and fear
That intellect flew outward, dispersed
In the gusting air and swam in a sacredness.

I climbed in a rainstorm as ancient
As the peak itself, my body a oneness
With the far beginnings of life—
The great heights of the mountains,
The great heights of the swirling dark clouds
And thin forkings and white jets of lightning.

No words are sufficient—
I cannot tell you what happened:
Only a man and his dog, climbing upward
To a split pinnacle where the earth ended.

And knew without words:
These mountains do not cry for tragedy—
They cry for peace.
They do not need us,
Do not want us,
Will applaud with claps of thunder
When the human race is gone.

*Numunana! I am the power, the power!*

Time without time, magnificent pulsings
Burned then in the nerve flares, imperceptible
Electric pulsings, perceiving, agonized sentient speck,
The human mind a billion synaptic crossings
Brought dimly to a moment's awareness and wonder.

I stood at the peak, under heavy clouds
And light bursts of rain, I stood,
A man with his dog, on the rough knife's edge
Of the Sierra Nevada, astride a final basaltic node,
And breathed the quick rain as it hissed on stone.

Sun! Set!

Westward the late summer sky blazed immense redness,
A scarlet mist enveloped the world,
Distilled from the air in fading light,
It dripped to darkness in the canyon clefts,
Life blood of the world revealed in that instant.

And light-flash, lightning, huge energy
Sparking from cloud to cloud, the dark pillars of sky
To the ghostlike giant peaks, titanic forms
That shouted to one another in years of noise.

Sunset.

And when the human race is gone—

*Numunana! Numunana lives in the Inyo.* . . .

## WAITING FOR RAIN

The canyons turn brown in early October,
Burned by the summer
And the hot winds
Of the year eating back on itself.

The stream runs dry in a rocky bed,
No longer fed
By the chill springs—
For the year is devouring its entrails.

Nor does the mockingbird flame the night
To melodic light
Beneath these thirsty stars:
The long year is changing its skin.

# INDIAN SUMMER

I awake one morning to find
That years have run on the wind:
Now autumn is here,
Yet summer refuses to die,
The heat persists, no tempering frost.

In the late morning I walk
By the pond, to the far side
Through a net of young willows,
Their leaves just starting
To yellow: and a hundred
Bullfrogs splash into the water.

Get down in the mud,
Little brothers: seasons turn fast.

Hot, dry winds leach earth,
And a touch of flame would send
Red waves through dead vegetation.

Late plums are shriveled on branches:
For all of this, the flight of the kingfisher
Suggests that winter comes sudden.

The white, drenching rains,
Then blizzard and wrenching
Of frost: the bare cirques
Of the High Sierra hunger
Snow, the rock hungers ice.

Little brothers, get down in the mud.

But I reach out now to the blast of winter,
For something within me hungers my death,
And my laughter cracks a clear, frozen air:

I race for the morning that finds
Such beautiful frost on the wind.

# AWAIT THE GREAT TURNING

Violence wrenches back life,
Yet the year moves slowly,
Slowly to the dark standstill.

The yellow and orange
Of autumn foliage persists,
A few leaves still cling—
No rain, warm days,
Hissing wind through brown grass
And dry thistle—even the cattle
Move slowly, inevitably,
Abundantly patient—patient.

Where now is last summer's vision,
When I stood daemon-possessed,
Astride the Sierra, and gigantic
Bursts of thunder
Roared through the gray cloud-waves?

Red hunger inside me demands
A great turning,
Yearns the year's turning.

I thirst for the dark sheets of rain.

## THE BEGINNING OF SPRING

It has been a cold winter. The eucalyptus trees
Are burned brown. The pond was completely frozen.

As the days grow longer and the warm rains
Pour down incessantly, catkins on the willows burst,
Daffodils push through the thawed earth, the plum
Blossoms are tiny clusters of eggs ready to hatch,
The grass curls forth, sensuous as a woman's pubic hair.

## AT THE END OF THE GORGE

I stand on the narrow catwalk of the canal:
Two hundred feet below, green water pounds
Through boulders, urgency of current,
To emerge against brilliant white gravel flats
Beyond the last sheer black cliff face.

It is springtime, red-centered trilliums,
Douglas firs tipped yellow-green.

I lean against the railing, look down at high water
Lapping the sandbar, am hurtled backward
Through seventeen years.

                    Nightime:
A half moon crouched on the canyon's rim,
While below a small fire burns orange—
I barely discern the forms of a boy and a girl,
Shadowed in firelight, lying together
On the moon-bitten sand, in the naked embrace.

Flute music, though perhaps they did not hear it then.

Innocent bodies rhythmed on the warm darkness,
A dance of nymph and satyr, unseen, unheard
In the soft, consuming whirlwind of years.

A jay screams. The illusion is gone:
Only green water that slows, begins to meander.

Instead I see the face of her daughter,
A child approaching womanhood:
Does she remember her mother? Distorted images. . .

For she who made love in the moonlight is dead,
Murdered, some fit of desperation,
A husband's jealous rage or impotence.

And I, who once lay with her by the fire,
In the white sand and the music we did not hear,
Am stunned by the dartings of swallows,
Odor of wild mock-orange, fierce April sunlight.

## MAY MIDNIGHT

The white goddess moves toward full,
Encircled by a faint spume of rainbow
In the mist of this warm May midnight.

The coyotes are quiet tonight:
No eyes gleam from behind
A screen of willow-brush and liveoak.

And yet I hear their laughter—
Coyotes laughing at the moon.

Tentacles of grapevines touch, reach
Outward, threadlike fingers of tendril
Cling, encircle, twine upward,
The moist crumple of new leaves,
Insidious delicacy, greensilver thin.

Now bullfrogs growl in the night:
I part the willows and stand by the water—
Eyes, eyes blinking at the pond edge,
Frogs crouched in shallow water,
They drift in the moon's undulations.

And growl: neither kingfisher nor heron
Will have them. Fierce, simple music.

Not even my presence disturbs them.

# COSUMNES RIVER IDYLL

Sometimes the realm of myth bursts
Into human lives—days when the sunlight
Touches the water of the river to silver
Fire—and the west-reaching canyon
Is tinged smoky blue. On such a day

A man and a woman
Grope their way into the rich brown
Darkness of a limestone cave,
Wriggle through narrow passageways
To the interior, sit in the cool,
The absolute blackness, walls
About them illumined only by the red
Glow of cigarettes.

                  And leaving
The cave, the suspension of time,
They move into yellow sunlight,
Wander upstream to a shallow pool,
Swim naked in the cold water,
Lounge upon a rock in the stream,
Or swim against the strong, subtle current,
Emerge to sit on the bank, drink wine.

And they will make love among
The shady rocks and the long, tufted grasses—
And afterwards watch the darting
Golden butterflies above reflecting water.

# FULL MOON IN AUGUST

Across the lake
A scattering of lights
And a faintness of melody
Over the darkened water,
The water lapping
At the stones on the shore—

Even the muted sounds
Of voices, the words
Indistinguishable
In the summer night
And the full white moon.

From the end of the road
One can barely see
The blur of a man and a dog
On the gray rise in the moonlight.

Are they waiting for someone?
Perhaps the man waits
For a woman,
Perhaps they were to meet
Secretly in the molten fire
Of the moonlight,
Perhaps they have even met
Here before:
One cannot tell. It is only
The shadow of a man and his dog,
A shadow that blends
In the silver-gray.

But across the lake
Are the lights of houses

And in the darkness one hears
The faint strains of music
And the muted tones
Of human voices.

While closer at hand
The night calls of screech owls,
The trill of their mating cries—
The alarm of a bluejay,
The sudden and unpredictable
Shrill of a mockingbird
That fills the night
With a burst of sweetness
And then is silent again.

And the sounds of water
Lapping against the stones
Of the shore, lapping and resting.

In the blur of the moon
And the odor of the liveoak
And the odor of grapevine,
One can see that the man
Is undressing,
The white of his body
More visible now
As he stands by the water.

There is no movement:
Neither is there sound.

# THE MOUNTAIN, THE HAWK

A chill wind was gusting,
Yet in moments of cessation
The late August sun
Warmed the gray spires of the peak.

A long summer had melted the snow,
And the low timberline foliage was dying—
We found a few flowers in bloom
Near the base of the igneous cliffs.

We descended, stopped to rest
At timberline on the north slope:
And a great hawk rode the blue air
Against the wind, furled his wings

And hovered mothlike above the dead top
Of a hemlock before lighting.
He tried to ignore us, then dipped
Forward to the wind and drank air again,

In perfect comprehension and mastery:
Curved away, upward against the still
Blue sky and over us—exploded to flame
In the afternoon sun, his wings crimson.

We came down from the mountain,
Would reenter the human realm—but cold wind,
And the infinite peace, the panorama,
And the great hawk burned in our eyes.

# RAIN FELL LAST NIGHT

The clouds eastward
Above the Sierras
Are white and gray
Against pale blue
As this autumn day spins toward sunset.

Dark gray
Close to the horizon,
So that I cannot see
The high range
Of the mountains: rain fell last night.

A sprinkle
Over the dull yellow grass
Of these low hills,
Patterning the dust
Of the roadway, orange-brown against yellow.

If only the clouds
To the east would break,
I would be able to see
The High Sierras:
I suspect that they're completely white.

# A BLOSSOM OF SEA AND NIGHT

A wailing of moonlight
Through fog, wave after wave
Illumined by mist,
A chanting above the water,
And Judith and I drinking wine.

Lights on the cliff above us,
Yellow smears in the fog—
They seem to move, gyrations
Of dancers, like insane dancers
Inviting the cold and storm of winter.

Shall we light a fire?
The driftwood of our lives,
Secret containment,
Even the firefingers that press together
In token of prayer as I blow
Softly into your ear, touch you
With my tongue and feel
Your body tense and then relax
In an upward drifting of smoke.

Across this wide cove
Another fire burns, flinging its incense
Back to us, the luminous shadows
Of dancers in a blossom of flame.

## JUDITH:

Your lithe body sings to my touch,
And I am bound to the mast
As my men row forward,
Their ears stopped with beeswax.

What bonds are these?
I break them.
Are you bound too?
Let me decipher those knots—
We shall move in blue-yellow flames,
Become one with the fire
In a dancing of blood and bright sinew.

# A MOMENT WITH NO TIME

We walked in to Proxy Falls,
A short walk, with autumn rain
Misting down from a gray sky,
The woods damp and puddles forming,
Bush maples flaring orange and red.

At the base of the upper falls
You slipped on a slick gray log—and fell,
Jumped up quickly, indignant
That I might think you awkward:
You would not take my hand,
Though I offered to help you.

But the lower falls were fascination:
Twin lace-like sprays cascading
From high above to the porous cinders
At the base of the volcanic cliff,
The stream absorbed to earth, magically.

The water, falling and yet not falling,
Frozen in a moving timelessness.

In the misty rain we gazed
For several minutes, then finally turned
And walked away, changed somehow
From what we were, released
From the bindings of our separate worlds.

And you said, "I feel as though I lived here once.
I think it was a thousand years ago."

That moment: joined us.

# IN CALAVERAS COUNTY

A dirt road, unused except by hunters
These twenty years: at the bottom of the hill
I park my pickup, shut off the motor,
Listen to the rain, see sunlight glistering
    In the clouds.

I walk in the mist and shining,
Through a meadow, the tall yellow grass
Of autumn, neglected apple trees with small
Red fruit. Among the drooping limbs
    The half-hidden shell

Of a 1930's automobile, growing back
Into the earth. And up the hill a house,
Portions of the roof sagged through, windows
Long since broken out. I enter through a doorway
    Time has burned silver.

A rusted stove and bits of linoleum
Still held in place by nails. The smell
Of decaying wood, a lingering odor of humanity,
Dim and vivid and damp. I know that a family
    Once lived here,

A man and wife, their son and daughter,
For I know something of their story. Debris,
Shards, the dampness of passing time.
Through the window I can see the old car
    Where children would have played,

The tall grass where they hid
From one another at summer twilight, the girl
Huddled amidst brackens, hardly breathing—
Thinking, "He'll never find me this time.
    This time I'll win the game."

Perhaps she would have thought
Of the two hills behind the house, separated
By the steep gully. "The bigger one's his,
I wish it were mine. Why is it his?"
    Then the mother's voice,

Calling them to supper, to a house lit
By oil lanterns, with cold water piped in
From the spring above the meadow, tea-kettles
Steaming on the stove, and in one corner
    The big tub for taking baths.

Sometimes when the girl was bathing,
Company would come. She didn't like that, was vexed
With her parents for being casual of her nakedness.
"Judith's in the tub again," the father would say,
    The visitors entering, laughing.

She would have been six years old
When they left the eighty acres and the apple trees
And the small house with thick-grown myrtle
Behind it, next to the road, the tendrils
    And the five-petaled blue flowers.

Yet the girl would remember. She would return
Sometimes—even as the years and the storms
Of winter pushed in the walls, took shingles
From the roof. Perhaps she would sit in her car
    After twenty years,

Would watch the darkness flow up
From the canyon, up through the black oaks
And the pines, would hear the lonely,
The oh so lonely wail of coyotes
    On the manzanita ridges—

Would strain to see what movement
In the tall grass where two children played
At hide and seek, a boy trying to find
His younger sister: some hint of motion?
Where is she hidden?

## NIGHT, MORNING,
## WOODPECKER RAVINE

It was past midnight when we arrived
At the cabin in the ravine: and the air
Was sharp with forming frost. Inside,
I built a fire in the sheetmetal stove,
And the room grew warm, dim-lit
In the flickering of candles. We talked
And drank wine and then made love
For three hours, at last let the fire die down
And slept huddled together, the downward pour
Of the flooding creek echoing the darkness of rest.

We slept through the early morning,
Were awakened by warm late autumn sun
And skies that had cleared. We drank coffee
And walked outside into a blaze of light,
The more welcomed after days of storm.

And found the woods on fire without flame—
Minute drops of moisture showered us
In a soft wind breathed down from pine
And oak: steam-smoke rose everywhere,
From the great oak's bole, from the brown mat
Of maple leaves on the path beside the stream,
From the silvergreen leaves of manzanita,
From the stream and rocks, this breath of earth.

We walked together beneath tangled grapevines
Until the upward slips of mist had burned our eyes
And nulled our voices: the thin, rising mist,
Everything smoking, steaming, totally alive,
Speaking, speaking to us. What was it saying?

# AFTER THE FLOOD

I:       The year draws now to the solstice.

To the west, across the great valley
And the Coast Range, the sky burns
A thin blue—but eastward
Dark-piled masses of clouds
Hover the long white Sierra front.

The red and orange and yellow leaves
Of the pear trees are fewer this morning,
Down with last night's storm.

II:       I dreamed before dawn.

A high desert, treeless, a rim-rock waste
But canyon-slashed by an immense river,
Flooding, gray-green water swirling
Out of its banks, the tops of canyon poplars
Still goldenleafed, emergent from the flood.

III.       She and I together, watching.

"Where does the river go?"
She asked. "It's not on the map."

And I knew then: "It crosses the mountains,
The earthquake changed its course,
It issues down the canyon near our home."

"We won't be able to return, then?
We'll love somewhere else."

"A dam has broken near the source,
But the water will not reach that high—
The land can bear its weight."

IV:      We journeyed through darkness half the night.

Arrived home under a star-filled, moonless sky,
Sank wearily to sleep with the sound of flooding waters,
Whir of wings. Dawn came and I awoke, walked out
Into bright sunlight. A huge lake lapped gently
Just below the house, intense silver light glittering
From the surface—I could not see across it.

Blue herons stood in the shallows: blackbirds
Swarmed and chittered in the willow trees.

# IN THE WHITE SILENCE

*The winter begins.*

Here, at the base
Of the mountains,
It will not be troublesome.
A few nights of frost,
Then the warm rains come,
And the grass seed germinates.

We stand
At the moment of the turning:
The days will grow longer now,
The imperceptible turning,
The huge yellow arcs
Of the sun will draw each day
Further northward:
The long day
Is defined by this present.

*But winter begins.*

And as a backlashed wave,
The cold storms will increase,
Drifts grow on the mountains:
The old ice,
Dormant, dwindling
Through summer and fall,
Will increase,
Will creep down the ravines,
Silently in the white silence,
Rock-chewing, gouging.

*The long winter begins.*

We are human—
And often we dance
Through many years,
The cycles, the alternations—
The dim, red sun
At the year's end,
The blue, searing force
Of midsummer.
The cold and the heat.

My thoughts travel north:
I see endless white forests,
The days short,
The streams ice-locked.
Even winter sun
In a blue sky does not disturb
The stillness,
The drifts of winter,
Great glaciers on the high peaks,
A continent spreading northward,
Still, barren, white,
A vast emptiness.

All light is gone,
The sun doesn't rise,
And no one hears the wind
Or the roaring
Of Arctic ice floes,
A frozen ocean,
Tremendous stillness, utter darkness.

Ice descends from the poles,
The mid-climates change,
Cities draw in on themselves,
The buildings unlit,
And corpses lie frozen in streets—
Human numbers dwindle.

*The time of long winter.*

Is it freedom—or death,
With the sun's fires extinguished?
Will the turning come,
Red tongues lick at the cold roots,
The pelvis shudder with pleasure?

Great Helios, we are your children—
We give ourselves to you
And dream your light,
We worship the rush of summer,
The love songs,
The warm, clear nights,
The couplings of male and female,
The owl's cry
And the kingfisher's dive,
The mating cries of coyotes,
Canyon-echoing cries
Of aloneness and yearning,
Midnight campfires
And the long shadows through trees,
Midsummer grapevines coiling
Their bright, phallic worship.

Do not desert us now—
Let the days grow longer once more
And the warmth follow
And the green explosion—
Your fire drive back the white fire
Of the bitter cold: we beseech you.

*Helios!*

# THE DRY WINTER

Drought year:
End of January, the rains have not come—
Black bones are visible in the white flesh
Of the High Sierra.

We pray for rain,
But the great Pacific storms sweep northward,
And the low winter sun burns meager grass
Sere yellow.

And drought inward:
Yet vision is cleared under winter sun,
The slow and relentless progression of years
Demands release.

Endure this distemper, break loose all human bonds:
Huge clouds hover the coast—the rainstorm comes.

## BELOW CHALK BLUFF

The Haywards: a mile-wide scar
On the hills, where diverted rivers
Could not slake the gold fever
A century ago. Now a pine forest
Struggles for life in alluvial sands
And gravels, huddles against clay
And aggregate cliffs where boulders
Exposed by jets of water find lichen
And moss and fern to cover nakedness.

Even now, after a century, the fever
Is here, hiding in cinnamon sands
And the carelessly piled heaps of stone.

Along an old canal, beneath winter sky,
A stunted black oak begins to think of spring:

Look at the color of the bark.

## GHOSTS AT MAL PASO

The long waves surge upon the coast,
Fling glitter-thin arcs of lace-like spume,
White, upon the dark beach at red sunset.

The fountain of the sun sinks back
Crimson through black fog banks out at sea,
Ellipsoid, flaring blood through hovering mist.

Here in the cove beneath sea cliffs,
Two ghostly forms crouch before a dying fire:
The woman rises, pirouettes, her quick feet

Singing across the damp sand, foam
Glinting red bites at her ankles—she dances,
Removes her clothing, tosses it up the beach.

The man rises also, then moves to her—
She retreats into the darkening water. He follows.
Waist deep, they embrace, a wave surges past them.

They scramble out of the foam. He lifts
Her and spins around: blurred forms gray against
Sunset: you cannot hear their secret laughter.

# FOR ROBINSON JEFFERS

I:   You were the master spirit: you saw through to the
     terrible agony.
Of God's self-immolation, the world-hawk that devours its own
     entrails
To give birth to itself in serene beauty.

You were the father: do your ashes sleep in the peace they
     desired?
The great waves still chew at the coast rocks, but human tenure
     is brief.
In the awful power of your lines, you pointed the way.

II:   I stare east toward the high, white peaks of the Sierra;
The tall wild plum is in full bloom, white, and white moths
Dance among the yellow mustard flowers. The sky
Is immense and blue, it leaps eastward from these greening
     foothills
And disappears beyond the far white rim. But here the wind
Flows on a soft steadiness from the south, bringing warmth.

III:   The dance of generation is patient and certain; it
     continues
All but imperceptible, fecund and lecherous. It knows the earth
Must be aroused, knows it is fearful. This wind will stroke the
     green thighs
And touch its tongue to the swelling buds, will not be satisfied
Until they all have flowered.

IV:   Yet now on the easy wind, two redtailed hawks have
     found a buoyant current:
They lie upon it, together, then apart, and once more together.
The sunlight burns their feathers into shining.

V:      I close my eyes to see a rain squall over the ocean,
            the vast glare of the sun
Sheening the blue-gray immensity of ocean westward from
            Pico Blanco, I hear the cries
Of the birds of the coast, shadows and brightness. I smell the
            good salt air.

VI:      This mild spring day, quite drunk with blossoming,
            obscures the long vision:
And yet there are storms to come, huge storms of human passion
And nerve-burning fire. The death-dance continues, the earth
            shifts slightly,
And the molten rock spews forth in red rivers; our promised
            land is before us
But the earth wrenches open, the granite splits.

VII:      You have peace. The daemon behind the screen of sea
            and rock
Has called you down—so now that angry spirit rich with patience
Threads earth where the big creek tumbles through orange-gray
            cliffs
To slip across the sand and join the sea: and now we seem to
            hear the hard old voice
In loving curses through the ever-restless waves.

VIII:      Far ages to come will pay you reverence: you saw to
            the mystery
And still loved it, you fleshed the bones of the swan.

# PORTRAIT OF WILLIAM EVERSON

The poet, tall, vital, strong in his early sixties,
Working with a bow-scythe, he shears lush weeds
By the edge of the dirt road at his retreat on Big Creek,
A glade amidst redwoods, an old fire station
In the Santa Cruz Mountains.

A large, gaunt man, the white mane of hair and full beard,
Intense, distant eyes, methodical sweep
Of the long-handled scythe, its rusty, curved blade
Honed to a fine edge and singing a swath through tall grass.

Odor of buckeye in blossom, morning sunlight,
Sea breeze, up through the canyon, through redwood and fir,
And as from a great distance, flute music.

Car on the road above, coming down.

The poet leans on his scythe, waits.

A young man gets out, Bible in hand, Fundamentalist missionary:
But suddenly uncertain, faced now with something that stirs
In the dark, pre-rational region—extends his hand, enunciates
The formal, memorized greeting: "I have come to bring you
        the word of God,
Mister . . . Mister. . . ?"

"Reaper," the poet says,   "Mister Reaper."

# THE RUINED CANE

—A PORTRAIT OF MY FATHER


Lightning jolted the sky from the north-east:
The on-coming tide of thunderheads heaped itself,
Poured down from the rim of the High Sierra,
And darkened the afternoon sky above the rich green foothills.
The wind grew still, the air thick and heavy to the impact
Of the approaching storm.

                            Bill Hotchkiss stood among rows
Of berry vines, intent on the coming rain. Dick,
His son, almost fully grown at seventeen, taller than his father,
Muscular, looked up at the swelling clouds
And then, quickly, at the older man's intensely quiet eyes.

It was very still: except that one could hear the leaves.

"I knew something was wrong," the father said. "There's always
Some bad weather late in the spring to take away half my crop.
This time it was patient—it waited for the new cane to make itself."

"Maybe you should have chickens again, Dad, and give up the
        berries.
Maybe the god is trying to tell you something."

The rain and wind both came at once: father and son
Stood in the berry rows and shielded their eyes
Against the stinging water.

                     "Son of a bitch, Dad, it's really
Coming down! Let's get in—out of this stuff."

The father did not move. "It was bound to come," he said.
"It won't be too bad unless there's hail. Hail will take off half
The first crop at least."

                                        They stood silently, in the rain,
Watching the green shoots grow heavy with water, wilt.
Their shirts were soaked, and little streams ran down
From their hair and across their faces. Thunder split the sky,
And sheets of bouncing hail drummed on the roof of the long,
Empty chicken houses, shredded bits of oak leaf out of the trees,
Ate hungrily at the berry vines.


                                        "There it is, Richard.
I knew it was coming."


                          The boy was shivering: "Come on, Dad,
Let's get into the house. Maybe Mom's got some coffee ready.
No sense standing out here."


                                        They went into the house
And ate fresh-baked bread smeared with butter. The father
No longer even looked out the window to watch
The pelting hail that continued to come in frenzied bursts.

The electric lights dimmed, grew bright again, and then
Went out. The mother continued baking bread in the wood stove,
And the father lit the kerosene lamp and began to adjust the figures
In one of his ledgers. The boy went out to the woodshed
And came back into the house with a great armload of musky
Oak wood. His mother quickly brushed the white flecks of hail
Out of his hair. "You never remember to wipe your feet,"
She said, even without looking to see if he had.

Two hours later a warm wind came on: and the sky grew quiet,
And sunlight drained down through the clouds. A small blue area
Spread out like fire, and the storm was over. Bill Hotchkiss
Closed his ledger, put on a red plaid jacket, and walked out
Once more to inspect his berry vines. Through the kitchen
Window, sitting in his father's usual place, Dick watched
The older man's gloved hands as they touched
And petted the ruined cane.


                                                            49

# THIS YEAR, THIS AGE

The skin on the back of my hand
Is thin and dry.

　※

It is impossible to know whether today
Marks the beginning of summer or of autumn.

　※

This is the year of the great drought:
The young buckeye loses its leaves
Even as the larger tree flares white cones of blossom.

　※

Our huge Aleutian storms
Did not spin south far enough.

　※

In my dream a gigantic black wave
Roils up from the ocean—then launches shoreward:
It sweeps over whole cities.

　※

The kingfisher perches on a low branch—
What lurks behind those small eyes?

　※

The rivers are low,
And the currents still dwindle:
Helgramite husks on gray rocks.

　※

Forest fires, like hungry red cattle,
Feed on the ridges.

　※

In the sere dust of August, Amaryllis blooms.

# A NUMBNESS AT THE HEART

I:      Vultures or hawks?

They spiraled against the gray autumn sky,
Gray without rain, without thunder.
I had never seen so many at once.

II:     At the hospital, we talked together.

I spoke of life;
You looked beyond me, you saw something else.

III:    A day later, words over the telephone.

"Don't expect too much."

IV:     My brother Dick met me at the college.

Two hours later I was driving up to Grass Valley;
I was aware, aware of what? A numbness at the heart.

V:      By afternoon I was home again.

A strange, dark, moving pattern against the air:
Moving in spirals, wending the currents of sky—
A congress of hawks and vultures,
Interpenetration, cyclone and anticyclone.

## BILL HENRY

My father. Summer has come again,
The first since you passed into darkness
And left me, your first son, named for you,
Looking forward to twilight.

Raspberry cane sways in the soft wind,
The red fruit swells out its clusters.

A rifle bullet in the mouth.

Hawks and vultures together spiraled the sky,
Against a grayness of autumn, that afternoon,
The last day we talked together.

I do not believe in omens. What did the omen mean?

Honeybees settle on the strawberry blossoms.

Two days later my brother was waiting for me,
In my office, at the college. "It's over," he said.

You were a wise man, a good man, a strong man:
You touched the red earth, things grew in abundance.

And that afternoon, again, I saw the swarming
Great birds of the air—more than a hundred,
Drifting in wide, lazy circles, drifting westward.

I do not believe in omens. Yet I saw them twice—

And the summer heat settles in. The Sierras burn dry,
The grass is yellow this year of the terrible drought:
Fire incubates its beautiful flowers in pine needles
And rotting logs. Only late rains will quench it.

Your rifle stands behind me, in the corner,
Metallic presence humming in the strawberry blossoms.

## SARDINE FALLS

Sonora Pass road, high meadows at the foot
Of Leavitt Peak, the glaciated north face:
We walk upstream, the morning air living
With bird song, the slough of ancient glaciers,
Volcanic debris, Jeffrey pine, sagebrush,
Aspen, and come to the foot of the lower falls.

We watch a pair of ouzels playing at the edge
Of the cascade. We think of spending a night
Here, wish we had brought sleeping bags.

Upstream, over a low rise of marshy ground,
Then to the base of the falls, where the stream
Pounds down through a three-foot split
In a huge basalt boulder. We scramble
Through loose rock, upward, to a grassy ledge
At the foot of the main falls: the stream's
Hundred foot plunge, the height turning the water
To white spray, wind whirling the mist
Against the sheer black face of the mountain.

Give us wings, we would dart through falling water,
Would build our nest on the highest ledge
Where the stream pours over, live in the hissing roar.

## FOR JUDITH

I:       How many times have we made love?

Let it be a billion: but one time
We must not forget, our first time,
Making virgins of us both.

II:      We drove down the bad road to Cosumnes River.

Parked the car, walked upstream,
Through boulders and wild grapevines
And willow tangles, along the river,
Climbed up the limestone cliffs
Where the big nutmeg roots to the rocks
At the entrance to the cave.

III:     I think you were frightened as we entered the darkness.

We were like children together,
Crawling back through narrow passages,
The intense blackness
When we turned off the flashlights,
Anticipating the sexual act, uncertain
When and where it would happen, but certain.

IV:     We left the cave, walked upstream a mile or so.

Dry summer grass, the buckeyes
Losing their leaves, the air still and hot,
We came to a pool in the river,
A shaded bank under mock-orange and willow:
And we drank wine, do you remember?

V:      We undressed to go swimming: you were suddenly very shy.

I felt clumsy, very awkward—
Stumbled in the water because
I could not take my eyes off your beautiful body;
We swam, I came up from beneath
To grab your legs—and we rolled and kissed
In the pleasant glare of the green water.

VI:      Then it was time, yes, and we both knew it.

We sat together in the bunch grass
Under the mock-orange and willow,
A little confused, and drank more wine,
Riverstones among the clusters of grass,
No place to lie down. My cock
Grew stiff with the blood of desire,
And I rolled you over on top of me
As I lay among the rocks and the bunch grass,
And we clung and moved together
Until our bodies were slippery with lovesweat.

## COYOTE SEQUENCE

In the white eye of the moon,
In the silver shadows of willow and bramble,
In the roiled-up manzanita dark:
A shrill chorus of coyotes.

You drive the steep road to the canyon bottom
And you see them:
Yellow eyes flickering among mulleins.

We hunt them with traps,
We leave out the poisoned bait,
We rifle them down with telescopic sights:
Yet they do not diminish.

A rabbit watches, hypnotized
As the song-dog plays with a stick—
And another coyote comes up from behind,
On tiptoes.

A gopher snake flows through the grass,
Stops, arches its head, the black tongue darting:
A gray coyote dances in the sun.

When the wolves grow few
And pace toward the long darkness,
Coyotes will mate with them.

A bush-tailed blur in the moonlight,
And all our dogs bark for an hour.

A cow drops a stillborn calf in the summer night,
By morning only hair and a few bones remain.

Past midnight they prowl along city streets,
Knock over garbage cans, kill cats:
Morning finds three young coyotes
Paddling circles in a swimming pool.

A meadow in the High Sierra,
Crippled fawn, the mother trying to protect it—
But a gray-brown pack closes in, the quick jaws.

Sometimes ground squirrels don't run fast enough.

Sprawled on a smooth granite boulder,
A coyote dreams in the afternoon sun:
And the pointed ears twitch.

My dog runs all night:
In the morning he returns, limping,
Small, sharp teeth marks in his ears and face.

Coyotes! Beautiful song-dogs!
You prance in the frozen December grass,
You dart across paved roads,
You raid the chicken-run,
Your midnight music echoes over the low hills.

Broken-backed, you smile at me as I pet you—
I promise you rabbits and squirrels, not knowing
The spine is severed—you let me stroke your fur,
You listen patiently, condescendingly,
Curious about human creatures, and wait for release.

You never die—
Your numbers increase—
The quick yellow eyes and the bushy tails,
The nimble, mysterious dog-brains,
The playful, tenacious spirits.

A fine pair of white ducks disappears overnight.

I walk through the warm darkness,
Under the liveoaks:
Something nips at my pantsleg.

The spring day was full of coyotes—
Switching tails, yellow eyes, the ripe odor of coyotes.

Across the high desert at night—
Coyote eyes, everywhere, miles of them.

In the crumbled ruins,
In the wrenched-down piles of stone
And the empty streets
Where grass splits open the concrete
And the tangled wire and rusted-out shells of automobiles
And the splintered glass,
Rubble that once was Los Angeles, Denver, Seattle,
Whole rivers of coyotes flow and wail in pure joy.

## ABOVE TIMBERLINE

Above the last twisting, wind-tormented juniper,
In a world where spring is followed by winter
And countless small flowers bloom when the snow melts
In July, burn dry in August, and the first snow
Gusts in with mid-September.

                                                And above even that,
The dark red spires of the mountain pierce up
Through the talus slope, and I climb the ever-diminishing
Surge of rock anchored against an overwhelming thinness of blue:

Thirty feet from the summit I find, etched back by storm
And thaw, a layer of sandstone, alluvial sand.

And know the peak of this mountain was once a lake bed,
Compressed remnant, this fragment of a vanished creation.

I climb back into the cleft, to the nick of time,
And run my fingers across the compacted grains,
Volcanic mudflow above and below, I touch the wonder of it,
I swim through primeval waters, struggle upward
Through greenness to a pattern of light on the waves.

And breathe the rank air of that ancient time.

# CLIMB TO THE HIGH COUNTRY

I: Some force, unknown to us, unanticipated, drew us together.

> In the wild orchard
> Where two streams flow into one:
> Thin, autumnal rain.

II: A flaring of passion, a mating of white violence.

> Storm-break: great cloud waves
> Pound the blue beach of the sky—
> Bright gusts of sunlight.

III: And are joined, the old moralities now less than nothing.

> We follow the stream
> Upward, past sheer waterfalls:
> We will know love, sleep.

IV: Images of life and death intermix, fuse the delicate wonder.

> Red-yellow sunset:
> Vultures stream from the aspens—
> Powerful, dark wings.

V: Cities will burn, great wailing throughout the land.

> A dying campfire,
> And above us vast star-swarms—
> We cling in the warmth.

VI: The long night passes, we sleep, then awaken with dawn.

> Deer glide by, phantoms
> In the dim gray morning light:
> She and I embrace.

VII: Terrible sadness drifts with the wind, strange music.

    Seepage from high slopes
    Where the late snow slowly melts:
    Pools glister brilliance.

VIII: We have left humanity and yet brought it with us.

    Uncharted forests,
    An eagle glides up the air:
    We climb our mountain.

IX: Something has happened on the plains below, poisonous.

    Westward the cities,
    Dim in the far blue distance:
    Brisk wind, the storm's past.

X: All things will be created anew, the same four elements.

    Wind sings in our blood—
    We drink rare wine together
    In this high, clear air.